Understanding & Overcoming Credit Card Debt

Roggie Clark

Learn How To Invest in Gold With This Book

Are you ready to take control of your financial future and explore the world of gold investing? Whether you're new to investing or seeking to diversify your portfolio, this beginner-friendly guide will give you the knowledge and confidence to invest in gold, and other precious metals.

https://www.amazon.com/Ultimate-Investing-Buying-Guide-Beginners-ebook/dp/B0F1KWWDXG

Learn How To Invest in Silver With This Book

The Ultimate Silver Investing & Buying Guide For Beginners is your clear, no-nonsense guide to incorporating silver into your wealth-building strategy.

https://www.amazon.com/Ultimate-Silver-Investing-Buying-Beginners-ebook

Learn How To Invest in Gold For Retirement With This Book

Whether you're approaching retirement or already enjoying it, protecting and growing your wealth is critical. Gold Investing for Retirement Security is your clear, no-nonsense guide to incorporating gold into your retirement strategy.

https://www.amazon.com/dp/B0F1MCB6V1

Learn Macro and Micro Economics, With This One Book

Whether you're a student, a professional, or simply someone eager to understand the world around you, this book is your perfect introduction to the fundamentals of micro and macroeconomics.

https://www.amazon.com/Macro-Micro-Economics-Made-Beginners-ebook/dp/B0DPHTFVQG

Copyright

Title: Understanding & Overcoming Credit Card Debt
Author: Roggie Clark

Cover Design: Roggie Clark
Editing: Renee' Clark

Printed in the United States of America

Disclaimer

The views and opinions expressed in this book are those of the author and do not necessarily reflect the official policy or position of any individual, company, or organization cited or referenced in the text.

The author is not affiliated with any of the individuals, companies, or organizations mentioned in the text, nor does the author receive any form of compensation for citing or referencing them. Some sample scenarios in this text are fictitious. Any similarity to actual persons, living or dead, is purely coincidental.

The professional information (strategies, tips, and concepts) in this text is provided on an "as is" basis, without warranties of any kind, express or implied. While every effort has been made to ensure the accuracy of the information contained herein, neither the author nor the publisher makes any representations or warranties regarding its completeness, reliability, or applicability. The information is for educational and informational purposes only and should not be interpreted as professional, legal, financial, or business advice.

This book does **not** constitute financial advice, investment guidance, or legal counsel. Any financial, business, or investment decisions made based on this book are done **at your own risk**. You should always conduct your own research and consult a **certified financial advisor, le-**

gal professional, or other qualified expert before making any decisions that could impact your finances, business, or legal standing.

Neither the author nor the publisher guarantees any specific results or outcomes. By reading this book, you acknowledge and agree that the author and publisher shall not be held liable for any direct, indirect, incidental, or consequential damages, financial losses, or harm arising from the use or misuse of the information contained in this text. You assume full responsibility for any actions taken based on the content of this book.

Table of Contents

Section I: Understanding Credit Card Debt

Chapter 1: Introduction

According to the New York Federal Reserve, in 2024, U.S. credit card debt reached a record high of **$1.21 trillion** (Federal Reserve Bank of New York). Additional analysis from CNBC found that this debt isn't confined to any one generation. Some age groups carry larger outstanding balances than others, with **Generation X** having the highest average credit card debt at **$7,155**, followed by **Baby Boomers ($6,043)**, **Millennials ($4,322)**, and the **Silent Generation ($3,177)**. **Generation Z** has the lowest average credit card debt at **$1,963** (CNBC).

At first glance, these numbers may not seem alarming. I mean, nowadays, who isn't sitting with some type of credit card debt? Rising **Inflation** and the **gradual decrease in the purchasing power of the U.S. dollar** has made it harder to afford basic necessities like housing, healthcare, food, and transportation.

In fact, things have gotten so expensive that it has now become socially acceptable to use "**Buy Now, Pay Later**" to finance a food purchase. Yes, now you can buy lunch and pay for it in installments. This sounds ridiculous, but when you really dig into the growing **affordability crisis** in America, it paints a clearer picture. The truth is, people are using credit cards for everything from groceries to rent and car payments, not just to make small or silly purchases. Our everyday lives are being financed.

According to the article, ***U.S. Credit Card Debt Rises as Housing and Other Costs Remain High***. Credit card debt, when coupled with increasing housing prices, can be to blame for the growing crisis.

"It's impossible to look at rising credit card debt without acknowledging the high cost of living, such as housing prices". Author Casey Quinlan says in her article, she continues, " The Consumer Price Index, a measure of inflation, showed that in July, shelter increased 0.4 percent and made up 90 percent of that month's rise in the all-items index" (Quinlan).

Ted Rossman, a senior industry analyst at Bankrate, who is quoted in her article, further explains:

> "Inflation is definitely contributing to higher balances. Even if it's a category like rent, which most people are not putting on a credit card, if you're getting squeezed on rent, you have less money to go around for groceries and gas and other things that maybe you are putting on a credit card now" (Quinlan).

Their words help highlight the growing crisis. But how did we get here? Credit cards were originally intended to provide people with easier access to financing. Instead of going to a bank and facing scrutiny over your **finances**, **job history**, **gender**, or **race** just to secure a small loan, credit cards offered a more accessible alternative. That was the idea.

Unfortunately, over the last decade—and really since credit cards became widespread in the mid-20th century—this financial tool has evolved into a **debt trap**. More than ever, Americans are relying on their credit cards just to get through the month. Politician Elizabeth Warren was interviewed in PBS's Frontline's 2004 documentary, ***The Secret History of the Credit Card***. In the documentary, she was quoted as saying:

> What families are discovering, even with mom and dad in the workplace, is they often can't make it to the end of the month, and so they often use credit cards to bridge the gap. They borrow to make ends meet. She continues with. And then what happens is, something goes wrong. Somebody loses a job, somebody gets sick, family breaks apart, death or divorce (Elizabeth Warren, The Secret History of the Credit Card, 13:21).

What she is essentially saying is that what was once reserved for emergencies has now become the only way people can afford everyday life. A safety net has transformed into a financial "Frankenstein". Research has found that "Neoliberal economic policies" may be to blame for this issue.

Since the 1970s, Americans—particularly those with lower incomes—have been increasingly pushed toward taking on debt. The deregulation and so-called "**democratization**" of the credit industry have made consumer debt more accessible than ever (American Public Health Association). However, this shift coincided with a decline in working wages, forcing many individuals to rely on credit not just for discretionary spending but for essential expenses like rent, food, and emergency costs (American Public Health Association).

These policies have been implemented and promoted by the financial industry, and politicians for decades, think back to **Reaganomics** in the 1980s (Wikipedia), so it is no wonder that so many Americans are drowning in debt, and feeling this sense of perpetual "**indebtedness**" that disportionally affects Black, Indeginous, and Latinos differently than White Americans (American Public Health Association).

Credit card debt is becoming a major issue for the future of our country, but in order to address this issue it starts on a microcosm level with the consumer changing their habits. **That means you**!

If you're reading this book, you're likely one of the millions of Americans carrying credit card debt, searching for a way out. Even if becoming completely debt-free isn't immediately feasible, I bet you want to at least learn how to take control—how to make peace with your financial situation and ensure that the debt no longer runs or ruins your life. Stop letting the credit card companies control your life and start fighting back! This book is here to help you do exactly that.

Last Thoughts

In this book, we'll explore the psychology of debt—why so many people fall into the cycle, how credit card companies keep consumers trapped, and how to overcome the emotional toll that debt takes on you. By the end of this book, you'll have the tools and knowledge to avoid getting into debt in the first place, and instead learn how to make the most of your money, and make real investments that build real wealth.

Breaking free from credit card debt isn't just about paying off balances; it's about shifting your mindset, understanding the system, and taking control of your financial future. It's time to take that first step. Let's begin with first going over the history of credit cards. This chapter will help you better understand how credit cards came to be.

Chapter 2: History of Credit Cards

While it may seem like credit cards have been a part of our lives forever, they are actually a modern invention based on some ancient, historical practices. Let's explore in detail the history of credit cards and how they came to be.

Ancient Credit System

The concept of credit has deep historical roots, dating back to ancient civilizations where lending and borrowing practices were formally established. In Babylon, the **Code of Hammurabi (circa 1792 B.C.–1750 B.C.)** set legal guidelines for loans, interest rates, and debt repayment, demonstrating the early importance of regulated credit systems (Experian).

> Historically, a loan was a financial agreement between a single borrower and a single creditor or merchant for a single transaction. Over time, some customers gained the option to "run a tab" with an individual merchant—effectively a revolving line of credit that can be continuously borrowed against and has no fixed payoff date. This is the equivalent of a modern store credit card that's not part of a larger payment network. (Experian)

Ancient Romans (circa 753 B.C.–27 B.C.) also engaged in credit transactions, credit was an essential tool for business ventures, and it's likely that nearly every Roman participated in some form of credit transaction (Wikipedia). However, credit transactions in ancient Rome were largely based on trust, and when that trust was broken, it often had a profound and negative impact on both the economy and the credit system (Wikipedia).

Credit Cards Begin to Take Shape

By the late 19th and early 20th centuries, the concept of consumer credit evolved further with the introduction of **merchant-issued charge coins** in 1865 and **charge plates** in 1914 (Experian). These small metal tokens, often bearing the customer's name or account number, allowed favored patrons to make purchases on credit at specific stores and settle their balances later. This practice became especially popular among department stores and fuel companies, laying the groundwork for more sophisticated credit systems (Experian).

The transformation of modern credit cards began in the early 20th century with innovations aimed at streamlining transactions. One of the earliest examples was the **Air Travel Card**, introduced in 1934 by the Air Transport Association in collaboration with American Airlines (Kandra). This card enabled frequent travelers to book flights on credit, making air travel more accessible to business professionals. Following this, in 1946, Brooklyn banker John Biggins created the **Charg-It card**, a localized credit system that allowed customers to make purchases at participating merchants, with payments processed through a centralized bank. While this system was limited in scope, it paved the way for the broader adoption of credit cards. (Experian)

However, the first widely recognized modern credit card was the **Diners Club Card**, launched in 1950 by businessman Frank McNamara (Seaman). The idea reportedly originated when McNamara found himself at a business dinner without cash, inspiring him to create a charge card that allowed customers to pay for meals at participating restaurants and settle the balance later (Seaman). The Diners Club Card quickly gained popularity, expanding to include hotels, entertainment venues, and other service providers, marking the beginning of the modern credit card era (Seaman).

American Express entered the credit market in 1959 with the first plastic card, initially offering a charge card that required full payment of balances each month (Kandra). That same year, Bank of America introduced the **BankAmericard**, a groundbreaking innovation in consumer finance (Seaman). Unlike previous charge cards, BankAmericard allowed users to carry a revolving balance, meaning they could make purchases on credit and pay off the debt in installments with interest (Seaman). This feature revolutionized the industry, making credit more flexible and widely accessible. The success of BankAmericard led to its eventual rebranding as **Visa** in 1976, reflecting its global reach (Seaman).

In 1966, a group of banks formed the Interbank Card Association, a cooperative organization designed to create a competitive alternative to BankAmericard. This association launched the **Master Charge card**, which later became Mastercard in 1979 (Seaman). The emergence of Mastercard and Visa established a competitive landscape that drove innovation in the credit card industry, leading to the widespread adoption of electronic payment processing, fraud prevention measures, and reward programs (Seaman).

Over the decades, credit cards have continued to evolve, incorporating technological advancements such as **magnetic stripes**, **EMV chip technology**, **contactless payments**, and **digital wallets** (Kandra). Today, credit cards have become an integral part of global commerce, enabling digital transactions across online and brick-and-mortar retailers.

So, as you can see, credit cards were once an almost harmless invention. A simple way to pay your debts when you are a little bit short on cash. But in the 1980s and 90s, credit cards would become a focal point of the banking industry.

The Credit Card Industry Expands

According to PBS Frontline, Sioux Falls, South Dakota, became a major hub for the U.S. credit card industry in the early 1980s, a transformation driven by both economic necessity and legislative strategy. At the time, the

U.S. was experiencing an economic phenomenon called **stagflation**—a period of high inflation and high unemployment, which hit South Dakota particularly hard due to its struggling agricultural economy and job losses. The state needed a new economic driver, and banking provided the perfect opportunity (PBS Frontline, "The Secret History of the Credit Card").

Banks across the country were facing pressure due to **strict usury laws**, which capped interest rates on loans and credit cards, limiting profitability. However, the **1978 Marquette decision** by the Supreme Court changed the game, ruling that banks could charge the interest rate of the state where they were headquartered, rather than the state where their customers lived. This meant that if a bank moved to a state with no interest rate caps, **it could charge higher interest rates nationwide** (PBS Frontline, "The Secret History of the Credit Card").

Seeing an opportunity, South Dakota acted quickly. In **1980, Governor Bill Janklow pushed legislation to eliminate interest rate caps**, making the state one of the most attractive places in the country for banks to relocate. **Citibank**, struggling under New York's restrictive regulations, became the first major financial institution to take advantage of this and moved its credit card operations to Sioux Falls in 1981. (PBS Frontline, "The Secret History of the Credit Card").

Following Citibank's success, other financial giants like **Wells Fargo, Capital One, and First Premier Bank** established operations in Sioux Falls, solidifying its reputation as a financial hub. Companies like **CAPITAL Services** and other credit card providers also set up shop in the city, further expanding the industry and solidifying Sioux Falls as the Midwest credit card capital.

Also, according to Claire Tsosie's article: ***Why So Many Credit Cards Are From Delaware***, seeing the success of South Dakota, Delaware followed suit and enacted the **Financial Center Development Act** in 1981, which eliminated interest rate caps, permitted various fees on credit products, and offered tax incentives to financial institutions. This legislative environment, coupled with Delaware's established Court of Chancery, known for efficient corporate dispute resolutions, attracted major banks such as **Chase Manhattan** and **J.P. Morgan & Co.** to relocate their credit card operations to the state. These initiatives transformed Delaware into the East Coast capital for credit card issuers and processors. (Tsosie)

With these legal changes, credit card usage starts to rapidly expand. However, as usage expanded, **credit card marketing tactics** also expanded with it.

Credit Cards Take On A Mind of Their Own

With Credit card regulations becoming more lax, companies began to see an opportunity to expand their business quickly. In order to boost profits, credit card companies began to shy away from "**deadbeats**" or credit card owners who typically paid their bills on time, and began to target "**revolving door**" customers who were constantly maxing out their credit cards and paying the minimum payment. (PBS Frontline, "The Secret History of the Credit Card")

Financial consultants like Andrew Kahr began to consult with credit card companies in the 1970s and 80s to loosen credit card restrictions by offering customers the ability to make low, minimal payments on their debt.

> Well, I convinced the client that instead of having 5 percent of the balance as a minimum payment, we should reduce that to 2 percent. It's a very dramatic change, less than half. (Andrew Kahr, "The Secret History of the Credit Card", 18:23)

Kahr realized that by offering **lower minimum payments**, customers would spend more, and therefore increase the company's profits.

> Having a lower minimum payment allows you to offer higher credit lines, which, first of all, makes your card product more attractive because people judge, even if they don't intend to use the whole line, they would rather have a higher line. The high-balance accounts will be much more profitable than

> the low-balance accounts. (Andrew Kahr, "The Secret History of the Credit Card", 18:57)

Additionally, Kahr recommended to his banking clients that a **0% interest introductory offer** on credit cards was a great way to entice customers to apply for credit cards.

> People were offering 12.9 percent interest for the first six months, 10.9 percent on balance transfers, and I convinced the client to go straight to zero percent as an introductory rate. It gave them a competitive advantage. It led to, of course, the others also going to zero percent. (Andrew Kahr, "The Secret History of the Credit Card", 18:57)

Even though Kahr knew that the rate could change to something higher, he still recommended that banks offer it to customers.

> When you're getting something in the mail several times a week that offers you zero percent for six months - they look at the headlines of the solicitation in the mail, they spend 30 seconds on it, and, "OK, I'm going to be better off at the beginning. They're going to give me something. They're going to give me a zero percent rate." People believe what they want to believe. (Andrew Kahr, "The Secret History of the Credit Card", 18:57)

Predatory Lending Evolves

Kahr's hunches would prove to be right, because these recommendations started to become conventional wisdom for credit card issuers. But on the flip side, his marketing recommendations helped open the door to **predatory lending practices**. Credit card companies started to make their **Terms and Conditions** statements that accompanied the credit card application form longer and more difficult to decipher. Additionally, the statements started to include "fine print" conditions, for instance, with a zero percent introductory rate, it could be changed to a higher rate at any time, without notice. (PBS Frontline, "The Secret History of the Credit Card").

In the documentary, PBS also spoke to Robert B. McKinley, the owner of Cardweb, a research firm that tracks the credit card industry. In his interview, he explained further about these new practices.

> Absolutely. They can change it all. It only takes 15 days' notice to make those changes. I mean, you could be offered a 5 or 6 percent interest rate today and perhaps get it. Two months later, that could be 30 percent. There's nothing to prevent the issuer from changing those conditions. (Robert B. McKinley, "The Secret History of the Credit Card", 25:08)

The introduction of **Universal Default** would also begin to pose a challenge for credit card owners:

> If you do miss a mortgage payment, you do miss a car payment, any other— it can trigger what is called a universal default. They actually have the right to change it if you miss a payment with another creditor, or in some cases, even if there's a change in your credit worthiness. In fact, you don't have to miss a payment. You don't have to go over your credit limit to be in default. You could, for example— or maybe your balances are too high. (Robert B. McKinley, "The Secret History of the Credit Card", 27:01)

Credit cards were beginning to take on a mind of their own. Things would begin to grow even more out of hand when, in 1996, another significant Supreme Court ruling further boosted the credit card industry's profitability while sparking a wave of consumer complaints. The case, ***Smiley v. Citibank***, much like the earlier *Marquette* decision, removed state-level restrictions—this time on the fees that credit card banks were allowed to impose. Here's what Duncan MacDonald, Fmr. Citibank General Counsel, who helped work on the case, had to say about the results.

> The late fees that were common across the industry, up until Smiley, were in the $5 and the $10 range. And the economic thinking was that there had to be

> flexibility to allow up to $15. But Smiley came along and took the lid off it, it went from $5 to $10 to $15 to $29, and recently, it's gone up to $39. I would guess that it's probably going to go up to $50 a year-and-a-half from now. I certainly didn't imagine that someday we might've ended up creating a Frankenstein. (Duncan MacDonald, "The Secret History of the Credit Card", 33:33)

It was clear that by this time, predatory lending was becoming the new law of the land. Credit card issuers were only out for profit at this point.

> ...We're beginning to see banks do all this tweaking, where they're changing the interest rates and raising fees, adding new fees, all kinds of— the way they calculate interest, setting the due dates on a Sunday, on a holiday, on the hopes that maybe you'll trip up and get a payment in late. It has become a very anti-consumer marketplace. (Robert B. McKinley, "The Secret History of the Credit Card", 34:40)

While lending practices such as these were becoming the new norm, there were two banks in particular that truly personified the new lending landscape that was taking place in the 1990s. Two particular issuers that come to mind are **MBNA** and **Providian Financial**.

MBNA (Maryland Bank, National Association)

MBNA was once one of the largest credit card issuers in the U.S. during the 1990s and early 2000s. The company was known for aggressive marketing tactics, high fees, and targeting subprime borrowers. Some of MBNA's controversial practices included:

- **Aggressive Marketing & Easy Approvals**: MBNA sent out massive amounts of pre-approved credit card offers, often targeting individuals who may not have been able to manage additional debt responsibly.

- **High Interest Rates & Fees**: Many customers found themselves with high APRs, sudden rate hikes, and excessive fees, especially for late payments or exceeding credit limits.

- **Predatory Balance Transfers**: MBNA heavily pushed balance transfers with introductory 0% APR offers, but often included hidden fees or terms that allowed them to hike interest rates after minor infractions.

- **Debt Collection Harassment**: The company faced lawsuits and complaints about aggressive and sometimes illegal debt collection tactics.

Bank of America acquired MBNA in 2006 for $35 billion and faced significant backlash for inheriting some of its controversial practices. Here's what Andrew Guile, a MBNA customer who was interviewed in ***The Secret History of the Credit Card*** had to say about them after his rate was raised from 8.9 percent interest rate to 19.9 percent, and his minimum monthly payments nearly doubled.

> They told me the first time that my rate had been raised because they found an occasion back in 1998 when I had gone 60 days past due on a competitor's credit card. And I asked them, "What in the world does that have to do with MBNA, especially being six years ago?" I said, "That has nothing to do with my account here." I mean, that absolutely took my breath away. (Andrew Guile, "The Secret History of the Credit Card", 28:55)

Providian Financial Corporation

Providian was another major credit card lender, particularly known for **targeting subprime borrowers**—people with poor or limited credit histories. They were involved in a massive scandal due to predatory practices, leading to regulatory fines and a tarnished reputation. Pat Wallace, who was the head of the Better Business Bureau in the San Francisco area at the time, helped field Providian complaints.

> The first thing that got our attention, of course, were the numbers, the numbers of complaints. Providian was involved in all kinds of questionable offers and policies and procedures and operations. (Pat Wallace, "The Secret History of the Credit Card", 37:17)

Pat continued by saying:

> Providian, for example, was accepting payments from consumers on their accounts, depositing the checks but not crediting the account for sometimes up to several weeks. What was the net result of that? Invariably, the consumer got a late charge. (Pat Wallace, "The Secret History of the Credit Card", 37:39)

Some of Providian's worst offenses also included:

- **Misleading Fees & Interest Rate Hikes**: Providian was accused of unfairly charging hidden fees and increasing interest rates with little or no warning, making it difficult for borrowers to pay off their debt.

- **Deceptive Marketing**: The company engaged in misleading advertising, often luring in customers with low initial rates or credit-building promises, only to hit them with massive penalties and high interest later.

- **Unethical Billing Practices**: A **2000 lawsuit by the U.S. Office of the Comptroller of the Currency (OCC)** and the **San Francisco District Attorney's Office** found that Providian was deliberately misleading customers about fees, minimum payments, and interest calculations.

- **$300 Million Settlement**: After facing multiple investigations, Providian had to pay over $300 million in fines and restitution to harmed consumers.

In 2005, Washington Mutual acquired Providian, and after WaMu's collapse in 2008, its assets were taken over by JP Morgan Chase.

Today's Credit Card Landscape

Both MBNA and Providian represented the worst of credit card lending in the 1990s and early 2000s, capitalizing on hidden fees, misleading offers, and excessive interest rates. Their downfall, lawsuits, and eventual acquisitions, along with the broader **2008 financial crisis**, led to sweeping credit card industry regulations aimed at curbing deceptive and unfair practices.

The most significant regulatory response was the **Credit Card Accountability Responsibility and Disclo-**

sure (CARD) Act of 2009. Signed into law by **President Barack Obama**, this act introduced a series of consumer protections designed to prevent unfair lending practices.

The law added restrictions on interest rate increases (Credit card companies can't raise interest rates on existing balances unless a payment is more than 60 days late), provided fairer payment allocation (payments above the minimum must go toward the highest-interest balance first, helping consumers pay off debt more effectively), no more retroactive rate increases (the new law prohibited retroactive rate hikes except in special cases like introductory rate expirations or severe delinquency.), and no more Universal Default. ("Credit CARD Act") The act also introduced protections for young borrowers under 21, requiring proof of income or a co-signer to obtain a credit card, preventing banks from targeting financially vulnerable students. ("Credit CARD Act")

Following the CARD Act, broader financial reforms came with the **Dodd-Frank Wall Street Reform and Consumer Protection Act of 2010**, which led to the creation of the **Consumer Financial Protection Bureau (CFPB)** in 2011. The CFPB was tasked with enforcing rules against deceptive credit card marketing, investigating unfair lending practices, and ensuring banks provided clear, upfront disclosures about fees and interest rates. ("Dodd–Frank Act")

Additionally, some states introduced further protections, such as stricter regulations on debt collection and interest rate caps on certain types of credit. In 2010, the **Federal Reserve also implemented rules to limit overdraft and debit card fees**, requiring banks to obtain consumer consent before enrolling them in overdraft protection. (Board of Governors of the Federal Reserve System)

These regulations significantly transformed the credit card industry, reducing surprise fees, misleading interest rate hikes, and debt traps, particularly for students and low-income consumers. While these changes led to more responsible lending practices, some banks adapted by increasing annual fees or reducing credit limits for riskier borrowers.

Additionally, newer financial products like **Buy Now, Pay Later (BNPL) services**, like I joked about in Chapter 1, are gaining popularity as alternatives to credit cards, especially among younger consumers. However, regulators are examining BNPL providers due to concerns about hidden fees, lack of consumer protections, and rising debt burdens. It's like credit cards all over again, but worse!

Overall, the credit card industry is at a crossroads, with **higher costs for borrowers, increasing regulatory scrutiny, and changing consumer habits** shaping its future. While banks and credit card companies continue to profit from high-interest rates, policymakers are working to create fairer lending practices, though challenges remain for consumers managing debt in an expensive economy.

Last Thoughts

Hopefully, by reading this chapter, you are able to thoroughly understand how credit cards came to be such a hassle today. As you can see, it is built into the credit card industry to make paying off debt harder. Because your large debt balance is seen as big money for a credit card issuer, and like I said at the beginning of Chapter 1, with the growing affordability crisis, paying off credit card debt is becoming a nightmare. But again, fear not, in the next chapter, we will go over in more detail how credit card debt works.

Chapter 3: Understanding How Credit Card Debt Works

Understanding how credit card debt works is the first step to breaking free. Many people get into debt without fully realizing how interest accumulates or how minimum payments are structured. In fact, according to a 2023 Forbes Advisor survey, **46% of U.S. cardholders reported that they don't know or are unsure about the interest rate on their card** (Pokora).

This lack of understanding can make it difficult to get out of debt, and as you can see from reading Chapter 2, the credit card issuers make it their life's goal to make sure that the Terms and Conditions are as confusing and hard to read as possible.

So no wonder getting into credit card debt is so easy, but in this chapter, we will break down the mechanics of credit card debt, the impact of interest rates, and how these factors influence your financial health.

How Interest Rates Work

When you use a credit card, you are essentially borrowing money from the issuing bank. If you do not pay the full balance by the due date, interest is charged on the remaining amount. The interest rate is expressed as the **Annual Percentage Rate (APR)**; the average credit card interest rate is **27.89%**, according to Forbes Advisor's 2024 credit card rate report (Coleman).

But this rate can vary depending on numerous factors, like your creditworthiness, i.e. credit score, the card issuer's policies, and even what type of card you have. **Airline (30.31% APR), Hotel (29.38% APR)**, and **Business (29.20% APR)** credit cards tend to carry higher interest rates, according to Forbes Advisor's credit card rate report (Coleman). While **Balance Transfer Cards (28.49% APR)**, **Cash Back Cards (27.98% APR)**, **0% APR Cards (26.65% APR)**, and **Flexible Rewards Cards (22.51% APR)** tend to carry lower interest rates (Coleman). This information is worth keeping in mind if you are looking for the best credit card with the lowest interest rate.

Additionally, the **Federal Reserve's key interest rate**, also known as the **Federal Funds Rate**, can also affect the interest rates charged by credit card issuers. More specifically, the Federal Funds Rate affects the **Prime Rate**, which is what banks use to help them decide how much interest to charge for consumer credit products like mortgages, personal loans, and credit cards (Dieker and Thangavelu). Typically, when the Federal Reserve interest rate increases, so does the APR on credit cards (Dieker and Thangavelu).

Compound Interest

Credit cards use **compound interest**, meaning you pay interest on both the principal and previously accrued interest. This can make debt harder to repay, especially with minimum payments. Since issuers calculate compound interest differently, total charges can vary. Once you carry a balance past the grace period (typically 21–25 days), interest is compounded daily—each day's charge is added to the balance, increasing the next day's interest. This cycle accelerates debt accumulation as you end up paying interest on interest (Leicht).

Example: If you have a $5,000 balance on a credit card with a 20% APR and only make minimum payments, you could end up paying thousands more in interest over time, prolonging your debt repayment by years. So that $5,000 dining room set might end up costing you $8,000 when it's all said and done.

The Minimum Payment Trap

Many credit card companies set a minimum payment that is a small percentage of your total balance, typically around 2-3%. While this might seem manageable, it is designed to keep you in debt longer (Like I said in Chapter 2, Andrew Kahr basically created a monster by encouraging credit card companies to offer minimum payments). When you make only the minimum payment, most of your money goes toward interest rather than reducing the principal balance.

Example: If your minimum payment is 2% of a $5,000 balance, your first payment would be $100. However, a significant portion of that would go toward interest, leaving only a small amount to reduce the principal. This means you could be paying off the debt for decades if you don't increase your payment amount.

0% Introductory APR Trap

Again, thanks to Andrew Kahr, many credit card companies also offer **0% introductory APR** promotions to attract new customers. These offers allow you to carry a balance without paying interest for a set period, usually 6 to 18 months. While this can be a helpful tool if used correctly, it can also lead to more debt if you're not careful because the credit card companies often don't tell you that once the introductory period is over, you will be charged the full interest rate on your balance.

The Risks of 0% Intro APR Offers:

1. **Deferred Interest** – Some cards apply all the interest retroactively if you don't pay off the full balance before the promo period ends.
2. **Encourages Overspending** – The lack of immediate interest charges can make it tempting to spend more than you can realistically pay off.

3. **Balance Transfer Fees** – If you transfer debt to a 0% APR card, you may be charged a balance transfer fee, typically 3-5% of the transferred amount.
4. **Higher Post-Promo Rates** – Once the promotional period ends, the interest rate may jump significantly, often to 20% or more.

How Credit Card Companies Make Money Off Debt

Understanding how credit card companies profit from debt can help you make smarter financial decisions. Their primary revenue sources include:

- **Interest charges** – The longer you carry a balance, the more they earn.
- **Transaction fees** – Every time you make a purchase, the merchant pays a fee to the credit card company.
- **Penalty fees** – Late fees, over-limit fees, and cash advance fees add to their bottom line.

Below is a more thorough breakdown of what type of fees and penalties they charge:

- **Annual Fee:** A yearly charge for having the credit card, often applied to premium or rewards cards.
- **Late payment fees** – If you miss a payment deadline, you can be charged a hefty fee, often $25-$40, and your interest rate might increase.

- **Cash advance fees** – Withdrawing cash using your credit card often comes with high fees and immediate interest charges.
- **Over-limit fees** – Some cards charge fees if you exceed your credit limit, though many now prevent transactions from going through if you are over the limit.
- **Foreign Transaction Fee**: A fee for using your credit card in another country or for making purchases in a foreign currency.
- **Returned Payment Fee**: Charged if a payment is returned, for example, due to insufficient funds in your bank account.
- **Balance Transfer Fee**: A fee for transferring balances from one card to another, typically a percentage of the amount transferred.
- **Duplicate Statement Fee**: Charged for requesting a paper copy of your statement.
- **Minimum Interest Charge**: A fee applied if the interest on your balance is less than a set minimum amount.

Now knowing what fees they charge, you can see why they encourage minimum payments and high spending limits—it's in their best interest to keep you in debt.=

Last Thoughts

It is very important to know how credit cards work and how the fees are charged, especially considering that credit card issuers are known to hide or make it difficult to understand the fees. The main reason why people can't get out of credit card trouble is that they just don't understand how the credit card system works. Also, they don't understand the business model of credit card issuers and why they charge so much in fees.

By understanding this basic information, you can avoid the high interest rates and extra charges that come with credit cards. In the next chapter, we'll explore the psychology of credit card debt and why so many people fall for it in the first place.

Chapter 4: The Psychology of Credit Card Debt

Credit card debt is not only a financial problem; it's deeply intertwined with psychology and human behavior. Understanding why people overspend with credit cards requires diving into emotional triggers, the influence of marketing, and the behavioral patterns that drive financial decisions.

The truth is that there's a lot more that goes into credit card debt than just the reckless spending habits a person has. In this chapter, we'll explore how these factors contribute to debt accumulation and how to break free from the cycle of credit card dependency.

Why People Overspend with Credit Cards

There are a lot of reasons why people overspend with credit cards. For one, credit cards exploit the **reward impulses** in an individual's brain, often leading to overspending. When one pays with credit, the brain's reward center—the **striatum**—is activated in a manner similar to drugs like cocaine and amphetamines, creating an expectation of pleasure (Shukla).

This neural response, combined with the illusion of **instant gratification** that credit cards provide, makes it easier to indulge in immediate desires—whether it's a new pair of shoes, a vacation, or a dining experience—without the immediate economic consequences (Shukla). The ability to delay payment fosters a sense of relief and pleasure, reinforcing the urge to continue spending, sometimes without fully considering the long-term financial impact.

Another reason is that credit card companies tend to play off consumers who have **insecurities** and a **scarcity mindset**. They sell to the consumer the idea that a credit card gives them more empowerment and convenience with making purchases, but in reality, it's an illusion that can lead to debt.

Also, the use of a credit card speaks to consumers who desire security should something go wrong, like an unexpected expense (medical emergency, car breakdown, birth of a child, etc.) or loss of income. So the person thinks that this credit card will be their safety net. Essentially, credit cards give the consumer a false sense of security.

Lastly, marketing tactics by credit card companies have also been shown to encourage impulse purchases. The introduction of tactics like "**Buy Now, Pay Later**" has been shown to be a powerful psychological trigger appealing to a sense of **F.O.M.O.** or a **Fear of Missing Out** (Prelec and Simester). When credit cards offer the ability to buy now and pay later, the decision-making process becomes less rational. The immediate availability of credit can feel like a chance that must be seized, even if it's not financially responsible.

On average, those who expected to pay with a credit card were willing to spend more than **twice as much as those who had to pay in cash** (Prelec and Simester). In other words, people are willing to pay a 100% premium for the convenience of purchasing immediately and deferring payment.

How Credit Card Debt Impacts Mental Health

In the previous section, we explored the psychological reasons why people overspend with credit cards. Now, we're going to take a closer look at the emotional and mental toll that credit card debt takes on individuals.

One of the most immediate psychological effects of credit card debt is **financial stress**, which can manifest in both emotional and physical symptoms. Studies have shown that individuals carrying high levels of debt are more likely to experience **psychological distress (**Pew Research Center), and psychological distress is often associated with adverse health outcomes, like **anxiety**, **difficulty sleeping**, and even **physical health problems** (Arvidsdotter et al.) These health problems can include things like **high blood pressure**, **obesity**, **inflammation**, **lower life**

expectancy, and **higher mortality** (American Public Health Association).

Another emotional burden is **shame.** Society often equates financial success with personal responsibility, which can make people in debt feel embarrassed or even unworthy.

> The inability to stay on top of payments can amplify feelings of failure or inadequacy, which can trigger shame. Shame often arises when we feel that we've acted in a way that goes against our core values. If we overspend or mismanage our finances, it can feel as though we are somehow failing as people. We might think: "I'm bad with money." "I've failed at something that should be simple (Astle).

This sense of shame can also prevent them from seeking financial help, leading to a downward spiral of debt and emotional distress.

Debt can also lead to **disorientation** and **hopelessness**, the debtor may find it harder to keep up with conversations or tasks, have difficulty speaking clearly, or making decisions. This can manifest in the debtor feeling like they are hopeless or are losing their will to live. They may even start to feel like they are seriously ill (Arvidsdotter et al.).

The debtor may also start to develop a sense of **denial**, which often manifests itself in behaviors such as not sticking to a budget, not opening bank statements, and generally not paying attention to money. This kind of behavior can make paying off debt even harder (Novotney)

Additionally, credit card debt, or debt in general, can **strain family relationships** as well. Research has found that **LFOs**, or **Legal Financial Obligations**, can lead to a longer period of homelessness for the debtor. Also, they can make it harder to keep up with things like child support, which missed payments have been shown to have negative financial impacts on children and mothers, as well as on the fathers' labor force participation and their involvement with the children (American Public Health Association).

Individuals burdened by debt may also withdraw from social activities, feeling ashamed or unable to afford outings, which can lead to **loneliness**, **isolation**, and **self-deprecating attitudes** (Arvidsdotter et al.). Overall, having credit card debt can take a serious toll on someone's life and overall well-being.

Indebtedness and the Socio-Economic Connection

Mentioning the immediate effects of credit card debt on one's life, I don't think it is enough to show the long-term impact of credit card debt. Research has found that the psychological consequences of debt tend to accentuate factors that are associated with falling into debt, so a sense of **indebtedness** becomes a self-perpetuating situation (Lea), this is important to consider because this sense of indebtedness and even "**Overindebtedness**" where an individual is in an astronomical amount of debt, is a serious social problem that disportionally affects people who are low-income and minorities (Lea).

Individuals identifying racially as **White tend to have greater access to low-cost loans and credit from mainstream banks**, which tend to provide greater economic opportunities, **while Black, indigenous, and other people of color (BIPOC) disproportionately bear the burdens of high-cost loans and credit and overindebtedness** (American Public Health Association). Also, credit reporting agencies have a tendency to penalize low-income and BIPOC individuals by making it harder for them to access lower-interest credit cards or other low-cost loans (American Public Health Association).

So again, when considering the psychological consequences of debt, it is important to consider that the emotions the debtor feels are not always self-induced; there are societal barriers that can prevent someone from overcoming debt, especially if they are from a, perceived to be, "unfavorable" socioeconomic background.

Last Thoughts

Understanding the psychology behind credit card debt is essential to breaking free from its grip. It's not just about the financial decisions we make, but also the emotional triggers and behavioral patterns that drive our spending habits. Credit cards, with their seemingly endless opportunities for instant gratification, often encourage overspending by creating a disconnect between the immediate purchase and the long-term financial consequences.

Marketing plays a significant role in fueling these habits, using emotional appeals and rewarding behavior to persuade consumers to swipe their cards without fully considering the price. Additionally, socioeconomic factors like income level and race also play a significant role in the likelihood that someone has uncontrollable debt. But by recognizing these factors, you can start to understand why these patterns emerge and how to fight them.

The key to overcoming credit card debt lies in changing the way we view credit. By developing a stronger sense of control, understanding our emotional triggers, and becoming more mindful of our financial decisions, we can begin to break the cycle of debt. It's also important to recognize that it's never too late to regain control and make smarter choices when it comes to credit.

In the next section of the book, we'll discuss how to assess your current debt situation and create a realistic plan for tackling it effectively, putting you on the path to financial freedom.

Section II: Overcoming Credit Card Debt

Chapter 5: Assessing Your Debt Situation

Before you can tackle your credit card debt, it's essential to understand the full scope of your financial situation. This chapter will guide you through the steps of **assessing your debt**, **reviewing your credit report**, and **identifying spending patterns**, providing you with a clear picture of where you stand financially. Understanding the depth of your debt is the first step toward creating an effective plan to regaining control of your finances.

How to Calculate Your Total Credit Card Debt

The first step in assessing your debt is to determine exactly how much you owe. This includes all outstanding balances across every credit card you hold. To do this:

1. **List all credit cards**: Start by writing down all of your credit cards, including the credit limit and the current balance on each one. If you have multiple cards, it can be helpful to organize them in a spreadsheet for clarity. Also, you might want to print out your bank statements as well to see which cards you've used and what you've spent money on.

2. **Account for interest rates**: Different cards might have different interest rates, so be sure to note these as well. This will help you prioritize which debts to pay off first (typically, the ones with the highest interest rates). Also, take note if any of your cards have any introductory offers like 0% interest, typically these are for a limit amount of time like 6 months, so be sure to check to see what the rate will be after the introductory period is over.

3. **Total your balances**: Add up all the balances from each card. This will give you your total credit card debt. The key thing to remember is to not be alarmed if you have a lot of debt, as long as you are aware of what you owe you can start to make a plan to get out of debt.

4. **Factor in fees**: Don't forget to include any outstanding fees, such as late payment fees, annual fees, balance transfer fees, or anything else that may have accumulated. These can increase the overall debt. Also, be on the look out for any hidden fees as well.

Once you have a clear total, you can start considering how to approach repayment, especially if the total debt feels overwhelming. When in doubt, just make the **mini-**

mum payment on all your cards, something is better than nothing.

Understanding Your Debt-to-Income Ratio

Your **Debt-To-Income (DTI) ratio** is an important figure that gives you a sense of your ability to manage debt based on your income. It's calculated by **dividing your total monthly debt payments by your monthly gross income**. This ratio helps lenders determine your ability to take on additional debt, but it can also be a useful tool for you as you assess your current financial health.

Here's how to calculate your DTI ratio:

1. **Add up your total monthly debt payments**: Include all debts, not just credit card payments. This includes any personal loans, car loans, student loans, mortgage payments, and Buy Now Pay Later agreements. Also, it may be helpful to consider recurring expenses like cable bills, electric bills, subscriptions, etc. Calculating these as well, will help you have an even clearer picture of your debt situation.

2. **Calculate your gross income**: This is your income before taxes and deductions (usually found on your paycheck). Also, if you do any side-hustles or have a small business you should also include the money

from those in your income as well.

3. **Divide total debt payments by gross income**: Multiply the result by 100 to get a percentage.

For example:

- If your monthly debt payments total $1,500 and your gross income is $5,000, your DTI ratio would be 30% ($1,500 ÷ $5,000 × 100).
- A lower DTI ratio suggests better financial health, while a higher ratio may indicate that you're over-leveraged and could struggle with debt repayment.

Reviewing Your Credit Report and Score

Your **credit report** is a detailed record of your borrowing history, showing how well you've managed credit over time. It impacts your credit score, which lenders use to determine your ability to repay loans and credit cards. Reviewing your credit report and score is an essential part of assessing your debt situation. Here's how to go about it:

1. **Obtain a copy of your credit report**: You're entitled to a free credit report once a year (every 12 months) from each of the three major credit reporting agencies: **Equifax**, **Experian**, and **TransUnion**. You can visit https://www.annualcreditreport.com/

index.action to get this score. Also, it's important to understand that these reports are just estimates, your real credit score or **FICO score** can be found at MyFico at web adress: https://www.myfico.com/ or you can find it out when you apply for a credit card or loan, but be aware that these things are a "**hard-pull**" on your credit score so it might go down because of it, so just keep this in mind.

2. **Review the details**: Your credit report will include information about your credit accounts (e.g., credit cards, loans), payment history, outstanding balances, any time your credit was hard-pulled, and any negative marks like missed payments or defaults.

3. **Check your credit score**: Your credit score is typically calculated based on your credit report, and it falls within a range from 300 to 850. Higher scores (700 and above) indicate better creditworthiness, while lower scores signal higher risk to lenders. Knowing your score can help you understand how lenders view you and give you insight into your ability to secure better credit terms in the future.

4. **Dispute any errors**: If you spot any errors on your credit report, such as incorrect balances or late payments that you don't recognize, make sure to dispute them with the credit reporting agency. Do

this by identifying the inaccuracies, then gather supporting documents, and submit a dispute letter or form to the credit bureaus (Equifax, Experian, and TransUnion) and the information furnisher (the company that provided the information).

The key thing to remember with your credit score is that it is not an indicator of who you are as a person, it's just a number, so use the score to gauge where you are, but don't allow it to run your life. Your credit score can drop for so many reasons other than just having a high debt load or missed payments. Sometimes your score can drop if you've **closed a credit line, if you've had too many inquiries, if you are not using your credit card enough**, etc. By simply paying down your credit cards, and having a long credit history you can improve your score.

Identifying Spending Patterns

In order to regain control of your credit card debt, it's important to take a close look at your **spending habits**. By identifying patterns in your spending, you can better understand where your money is going and how to make adjustments. Here's how to evaluate your spending patterns:

1. **Track your expenses**: Start by tracking all of your purchases for at least one month. You can do this manually or use an app to automatically categorize your spending.

2. **Categorize your spending**: Break your spending down into categories such as groceries, dining out, transportation, entertainment, and non-essential items (e.g., clothing, gadgets).

3. **Identify areas for improvement**: Look for areas where you're overspending. Are you buying takeout multiple times a week? Is shopping for clothes or gadgets a regular habit? Identifying these areas gives you the opportunity to reduce unnecessary spending and redirect those funds toward paying down your debt.

4. **Look for emotional spending triggers**: In some cases, spending may be driven by emotions such as stress, boredom, or a desire for **instant gratification**. Understanding these triggers can help you avoid impulsive purchases that could worsen your debt situation.

Last Thoughts

Assessing your debt situation is a crucial first step in regaining control of your finances. It may feel overwhelming at first, but by breaking down your credit card debt, understanding your debt-to-income ratio, reviewing your credit report and score, and identifying spending patterns, you create a clear and actionable path toward financial recovery.

While it's easy to get lost in the numbers and the complexities of your debt, remember that every step you take in assessing your situation brings you closer to understanding how to make better financial decisions. By recognizing the scope of your debt and acknowledging your spending habits, you set yourself up to create a realistic plan for paying down debt and avoiding future financial pitfalls.

Chapter 6: Strategies to Pay Off Credit Card Debt

Once you have assessed your debt situation, the next step is to take action. In this chapter, we'll explore several strategies to help you pay down credit card debt, from popular repayment methods to tools that can make the process more manageable. Whether you're looking for a method to organize your payments or a way to reduce the interest you're paying, there are options that can help you regain control of your financial life.

The Debt Snowball Method vs. Debt Avalanche Method

When it comes to paying off credit card debt, there are two primary strategies that people use to tackle their balances: the **debt snowball method** and the **debt avalanche method**. Both methods are designed to help you eliminate your debt, but they approach the task differently.

Debt Snowball Method: The debt snowball method involves focusing on paying off your smallest balance first, regardless of the interest rate. Once the smallest debt is paid off, you move on to the next smallest, and so on, gradually working your way to larger balances. **This method can be highly motivating for individuals who need quick wins to build momentum**. As each debt is paid off, the amount you can put toward the next debt increases—just like a snowball gaining size as it rolls downhill.

- **Pros**:
  - Offers quick wins, which can help keep you motivated.
  - Simple and straightforward to follow.
  - Helps build confidence by eliminating small debts early on.
- **Cons**:
  - May result in paying more interest over time because larger debts with higher interest rates are paid off last.

Debt Avalanche Method: The debt avalanche method involves focusing on paying off your debt with the highest interest rate first, while making minimum payments on all other debts. Once the high-interest debt is paid off, you move on to the next highest, and so on. This method saves you the most money in interest over time, as it reduces the amount of interest you pay overall.

- **Pros**:
    - Saves money on interest over time.
    - More financially efficient.
- **Cons**:
    - Can take longer to see results if your highest-interest debts are large, which may be less motivating for some people.

Both methods can be effective; it's just a matter of choosing the one that aligns with your personality and financial goals. If you need quick wins to stay motivated, the debt snowball method may be the right choice. But if you want to minimize interest payments and are okay with taking a bit longer to see progress, the debt avalanche method may be the better option.

Balance Transfer Cards – Pros and Cons

A **balance transfer card** allows you to transfer high-interest credit card balances to a new card with a lower interest rate, sometimes even 0% for an introductory period. This can give you a chance to pay down your debt faster by avoiding the compounding interest.

- **Pros**:
  - Can save you money on interest, especially if you qualify for a 0% introductory APR offer.
  - Consolidates multiple credit card debts into one payment, making it easier to manage.
  - Allows you to focus on paying down the principal without the distraction of high interest.
- **Cons**:
  - Introductory 0% APR offers are typically only for a limited time (6–18 months), after which a higher interest rate may apply.
  - Balance transfer fees (usually 3–5% of the amount transferred) can add to your debt.
  - If you don't pay off the balance before the introductory period ends, you could be hit with retroactive interest charges on the transferred balance.

Balance transfer cards can be a great tool for consolidating debt and reducing interest, but they work best for people who have a plan to pay off the balance before the introductory period ends.

Negotiating with Credit Card Companies for Lower Interest Rates

If you've been struggling to keep up with credit card payments, one strategy you may not have considered is negotiating directly with your credit card company for a lower interest rate. Credit card companies would rather work with you to ensure you stay on track with payments rather than risk losing you as a customer.

Here's how to negotiate effectively:

1. **Prepare your case**: Have a clear understanding of your current financial situation. If you've been a customer in good standing, use this as leverage. Be ready to explain why a lower rate will help you pay down the balance faster.

2. **Call your issuer**: Be polite but firm when speaking with the representative. Let them know you're interested in a lower interest rate and ask if there are any available offers or adjustments they can make to your account.

3. **Be persistent**: If the first representative is unwilling to help, ask to speak to a supervisor or try calling again. Different representatives may offer different solutions.

While not all credit card companies will agree to lower your rate, it's worth trying, especially if you've been a long-term customer with a positive payment history.

Consolidation Loans – When They Make Sense

A **consolidation loan** is a personal loan that allows you to combine multiple debts into one loan with a potentially lower interest rate. This can simplify your payments and potentially save you money in interest over time.

- **Pros**:
    - One fixed payment each month, making it easier to manage.
    - May offer a lower interest rate than your current credit cards.
    - Can improve your credit score by reducing your credit utilization.
- **Cons**:

- May require good credit to qualify for favorable terms.
- The loan may have fees or origination costs.
- Typically require proof of income, or an employer's information.
- If you don't stop using your credit cards, you may end up accumulating new debt while still paying off the loan.

Consolidation loans can be an excellent option for those with multiple high-interest debts and a good credit score, but they require discipline to ensure that you don't accrue new debt after consolidating.

Last Thoughts

Paying off credit card debt requires strategy, commitment, and the willingness to make sacrifices in the short term for long-term financial freedom. Whether you choose the debt snowball method for quick wins or the debt avalanche method to minimize interest payments, it's important to stay focused on your goals and be patient with the process.

Consider all the tools at your disposal—from balance transfer cards to consolidation loans—and weigh their pros and cons carefully to find what works best for you. In many cases, negotiating a lower interest rate with your credit card company can also provide significant relief.

Remember, breaking free from credit card debt isn't just about paying down balances—it's about reshaping your financial habits and taking control of your future. With the right strategies and a steady commitment, you can pay off your debt and create a healthier financial life.

Chapter 7: Avoiding Credit Card Traps in the Future

Once you've tackled your credit card debt, it's crucial to ensure you don't fall back into old habits. Credit cards, while incredibly useful, can also be a double-edged sword. In this chapter, we'll explore strategies for using credit cards responsibly, recognizing predatory lending tactics, and understanding the intricacies of credit card rewards—all in a way that helps you avoid debt traps and build a solid financial future.

How to Use Credit Cards Responsibly

Using credit cards responsibly is all about creating habits that foster financial health. Here are some key guidelines:

1. **Pay your bill in full every month**: The most effective way to avoid interest and debt buildup is to pay off your balance in full each month. This ensures you're not paying interest on your purchases, and it helps keep your credit score high. If this is not always possible, then try to make as large of a payment as you can to avoid high interest.

2. **Stay within your limit**: It's easy to get carried away when you have a credit limit to work with, but sticking to a budget and not charging more than you

can afford to pay off ensures that you're not overspending.

3. **Track your spending**: Keeping a close eye on your credit card purchases and how much you're charging helps you avoid spending more than you can repay. Many credit cards offer apps or online services that allow you to set alerts for your spending or due dates.

4. **Only use credit for essential purchases**: Using your credit card for big-ticket or non-essential items may feel like a quick fix, but it can lead to debt if you don't budget for it. Use your credit card for items you can pay off quickly—like gas, groceries, or other necessary expenses.

5. **Set up automatic payments**: To avoid missing payments and incurring fees, consider setting up automatic payments for at least the minimum payment each month. If possible, pay more to reduce your balance quicker.

Recognizing Predatory Lending and High-Interest Traps

We already went over predatory lending practices in great detail in Chapter 2, but here's a refresher of what these practices are so you can spot them and avoid them.

Here's how to recognize predatory lending practices and avoid falling into high-interest traps:

1. **Watch for high-interest rates after introductory offers**: While a 0% APR offer for 12 months might sound appealing, many cards quickly raise the interest rate once the promotional period ends. Make sure you're aware of the terms after the introductory period and try to pay off the balance before the rate increases.

2. **Look for hidden fees**: Some cards may charge excessive fees for things like late payments, balance transfers, or cash advances. Read the fine print to avoid surprises that can add to your debt.

3. **Check for universal default clauses**: Some credit card companies have Universal Default clauses, which allow them to raise your interest rate if you miss a payment with another lender. Be aware of this when signing up for a new card.

4. **Avoid unnecessary credit card offers**: While new offers for credit cards with rewards or low-interest rates may seem appealing, carefully evaluate whether you actually need another card or if it will simply lead to more debt.

5. **Evaluate a bank's reputation before opening a card**: Thanks to the internet you can easily do research on any bank you are thinking about getting a card from. Check forums, check reviews, ask questions, and evaluate multiple offers to ensure that you not only get the card with the best perks, but also to ensure in the event that something goes wrong you can get the proper customer support you need.

When (and If) You Should Close a Credit Card

There's often debate about whether it's better to close credit card accounts once they're paid off. The decision largely depends on your specific financial situation, but here are some considerations to help you make an informed choice:

1. **Impact on credit score**: Closing a credit card can impact your credit score by reducing your available credit and increasing your credit utilization ratio. A higher credit utilization ratio could negatively affect your score. However, if the card has an annual fee, encourages overspending, or has too high of interest rate – closing it may be a wise choice.

2. **Avoiding temptation**: If a credit card tempts you to overspend or is no longer serving your needs, closing it may help you avoid accumulating more debt.

Just be sure to pay off the balance first.

3. **Credit history**: The length of your credit history plays a role in your credit score. If the card you're considering closing has been open for many years, think twice before canceling it, as it could affect the length of your credit history and reduce your credit score.

4. **Consider downgrading instead**: Some credit card companies allow you to downgrade to a no-annual-fee version of the same card, which can help you maintain your credit history without paying for features you no longer need.

Understanding Credit Card Rewards Without Going Into Debt

Credit card rewards can be a fantastic benefit when used correctly, but they can quickly become a trap if you're using your credit card to rack up rewards without the ability to pay off your balance. Here's how to make the most of your rewards while avoiding debt:

1. **Use rewards cards for purchases you already make**: To ensure that you're not overspending to earn rewards, use your rewards cards for everyday purchases like groceries, gas, or bills that you can

pay off in full each month.

2. **Avoid high-interest debt for rewards**: The rewards you earn from a credit card are often not worth the cost of carrying high-interest debt. If you're not able to pay off the balance in full each month, consider skipping the rewards program or using a card with a lower interest rate instead.

3. **Understand the rewards structure**: Credit card companies offer different reward systems—cash back, travel points, or merchandise—and each comes with its own rules. Make sure you understand how rewards are earned and redeemed, and avoid chasing rewards for purchases you don't need or can't afford.

4. **Pay off your balance to maximize rewards**: To truly benefit from credit card rewards, you need to pay off your balance in full every month. Otherwise, the interest you pay on your balance will likely outweigh the rewards you earn.

Last Thoughts

As you move forward in your financial journey, it's essential to maintain responsible credit card habits to avoid falling back into debt. By using credit cards responsibly, recognizing predatory lending practices, and understanding how rewards work without falling into debt traps, you can enjoy the benefits of credit cards without the financial burden they can bring. Now, let's get into the last chapter.

Chapter 8: Final Steps to Financial Freedom

Achieving freedom from credit card debt is a major accomplishment, but the work doesn't stop there. True financial freedom is a continuous journey that involves restoring your credit, maintaining a healthy financial mindset, and growing wealth. This chapter will explore the final steps to ensure that you not only stay debt-free but also build a solid foundation for long-term financial success.

Restoring Your Credit Score After Paying Off Debt

One of the most immediate benefits of paying off credit card debt is the positive impact it has on your credit score. However, if you've had high levels of debt or missed payments in the past, it may take some time to fully restore your credit. Here are a few steps you can take to accelerate the process:

1. **Review your credit report**: After paying off your debt, check your credit report to ensure that all accounts reflect a zero balance. If there are any discrepancies, dispute them immediately to prevent errors from affecting your score.

2. **Make on-time payments**: Your payment history is one of the most significant factors in determining

your credit score. Continue making on-time payments for all of your bills to rebuild trust with lenders and creditors.

3. **Reduce credit utilization**: Even after paying off your debt, it's important to keep your credit utilization ratio low. Aim for using no more than 30% of your available credit. If you're using less than that, your credit score will benefit.

4. **Consider a secured credit card**: If your credit score is still recovering, consider using a **secured credit card** to help rebuild it. Make small purchases each month and pay off the balance in full to show responsible credit usage.

5. **Avoid opening too many new accounts**: Each time you apply for a credit card or loan, a **hard inquiry** is made on your credit report, which can temporarily lower your score. Be cautious when applying for new credit and only do so when absolutely necessary.

Maintaining a Debt-Free Mindset

Once you've paid off your credit card debt, it's essential to maintain the mindset that helped you get there. A debt-free mindset is one that prioritizes financial stability and avoids slipping back into old habits. Here are some key ways to maintain that mindset:

1. **Set clear financial goals**: Establish short-term and long-term financial goals to keep yourself motivated. Whether it's saving for a home, building an emergency fund, or starting an investment portfolio, having clear goals will help keep you focused on the future.

2. **Avoid lifestyle inflation**: As your financial situation improves, resist the urge to increase your spending just because you now have more available funds. Stay disciplined and allocate any extra income towards savings or investments instead of luxuries.

3. **Be mindful of your spending**: Continue to track your spending and avoid impulse purchases. Maintain a budget to ensure that your lifestyle remains within your means, and always be conscious of how much you're spending on non-essential items.

4. **Seek out support**: Surround yourself with individuals who have a similar financial mindset. Join online communities, attend financial workshops, or work with a financial advisor to keep your focus on staying debt-free and building wealth.

Keeping Up With Financial Education

Financial literacy is key to ensuring that you continue on the path to financial freedom. The more you learn about managing money, investing, and building wealth, the more empowered you'll be to make informed decisions that align with your goals. Here are some ways to continue your financial education:

1. **Read books and articles**: Continue reading personal finance books, articles, and blogs to stay informed about the latest strategies for wealth-building and financial management.

2. **Take courses or attend seminars**: Online courses, webinars, and in-person seminars are a great way to deepen your understanding of personal finance, investing, and even advanced topics like tax planning and real estate.

3. **Listen to podcasts**: Financial podcasts are an excellent way to stay updated on financial news, gain insights from experts, and hear real-life success stories that can inspire you.

4. **Work with a financial advisor**: If you're ready to take your finances to the next level, consider working with a financial advisor who can provide personalized advice on budgeting, saving, investing, and planning for retirement.

Investing and Growing Wealth Instead of Relying on Credit

Once you've paid off your debt and restored your credit, it's time to shift your focus toward building wealth. Instead of relying on credit cards to make purchases, you can now rely on your savings and investments. Here are a few ways to start growing your wealth:

1. **Start building an emergency fund**: The first step to financial security is having an emergency fund that covers 3-6 months' worth of living expenses. This will give you peace of mind and prevent you from relying on credit cards in case of an unexpected expense.

2. **Invest for the future**: Once you've built up your emergency fund, it's time to start investing. You may want to think about opening a business, or diversifying your investments with stocks, bonds, and real estate.

3. **Automate your savings and investments**: Set up automatic transfers to savings and investment accounts to ensure that you consistently put money aside. Automation removes the temptation to spend

what you should be saving.

4. **Diversify your income streams**: Look for ways to diversify your income. Whether it's through a side hustle, rental properties, or passive income streams like dividend-paying stocks, having multiple income sources can help you build wealth faster.

Last Words

Congratulations on completing this journey toward financial freedom. Paying off credit card debt and rebuilding your financial life is no easy feat, but it's one of the most rewarding things you can do for yourself and your future.

As you move forward, remember that financial freedom is not a destination—it's a continuous journey. By maintaining a debt-free mindset, continuing your financial education, and investing in your future, you're setting yourself up for a life of security, growth, and wealth. You've taken the crucial steps to break free from debt, and now, with discipline, patience, and knowledge, you have the tools to thrive financially.

I hope this book helps you with achieving a better financial state, good luck!

About the Author

Roggie "Raj" Clark is an entrepreneur and a 10-year marketing professional with a proven track record in e-commerce and digital business growth. Having built and managed successful online stores with thousands of sales and consulted for numerous marketing clients, Roggie has mastered the intricacies of online marketing, branding, and consumer behavior. He has also written several popular books on digital marketing, SEO (search engine optimization), and programming (HTML, CSS, and JavaScript).

As a former marketing manager at a fintech company—a role he secured through his own marketing and financial expertise—Roggie gained firsthand experience in financial strategy and wealth-building. This journey inspired him to share insights with amateur investors, helping them save money, make smarter financial decisions, and build long-term wealth. Raj currently lives in Maryland with his sister and niece.

Reference

American Public Health Association. *The Impacts of Individual and Household Debt on Health and Well-Being*. 26 Oct. 2021, www.apha.org/policies-and-advocacy/public-health-policy-statements/policy-database/2022/01/07/the-impacts-of-individual-and-household-debt-on-health-and-well-being. Accessed 3 Apr. 2025.

Arvidsdotter, T., et al. "Understanding Persons with Psychological Distress in Primary Health Care." *Scandinavian Journal of Caring Sciences*, vol. 30, no. 4, 2016, pp. 687–694, https://doi.org/10.1111/scs.12289.

Astle, Nathan. *Overcoming the Shame of Credit Card Debt*. *Psychology Today*, 2 Feb. 2025, www.psychologytoday.com/us/blog/the-psychology-of-debt/202502/overcoming-the-shame-of-credit-card-debt. Accessed 3 Apr. 2025.

Board of Governors of the Federal Reserve System. "Federal Reserve Board Approves Final Rule to Protect Credit Card Users from Unfair Rate Increases." *Federal Reserve*, 12 Nov. 2009, https://www.federalreserve.gov/newsevents/pressreleases/bcreg20091112a.htm.

Coleman, Evan. "Average Credit Card Interest Rate." *Forbes Advisor*, n.d., https://www.forbes.com/advisor/credit-cards/average-credit-card-interest-rate/. Accessed 2 Apr. 2025.

CNBC Select. "Average Credit Card Debt by Age." *CNBC*, https://www.cnbc.com/select/average-credit-card-debt-by-age/. Accessed 31 Mar. 2025.

"Credit CARD Act of 2009." Wikipedia, The Free Encyclopedia, Wikimedia Foundation, 1 Apr. 2025, https://en.wikipedia.org/wiki/Credit_CARD_Act_of_2009.

Dieker, Nicole, and Poonkulali Thangavelu. "How Does the Prime Interest Rate Affect You?" *Bankrate*, 17 May 2024, https://www.bankrate.com/credit-cards/zero-interest/how-prime-interest-rate-may-affect-your-monthly-bills/. Accessed 2 Apr. 2025.

Kandra, Kathryn. "A Brief History of Credit Cards." *Ellipse*, 9 July 2024, www.ellipse.la/post/a-brief-history-of-credit-cards. Accessed 3 Apr. 2025.

Lea, Stephen E. G. "Psychological Effects of Debt on Mental Health and Well-Being." *Social and Personality Psychology Compass*, vol. 9, no. 11, 2015, pp. 583–596, https://doi.org/10.1111/sipr.12074. Accessed 3 Apr. 2025.

Leicht, Angelica. "How Are Credit Card Interest Charges Compounded?" *CBS News*, 16 Dec. 2024, https://www.cbsnews.com/news/how-are-credit-card-interest-charges-compounded/. Accessed 2 Apr. 2025.

Novotney, Amy. "Debt and Mental Health: What We Know and What We Need to Know." *APA Psychology Grad Psych*, Jan. 2013, www.apa.org/gradpsych/2013/01/debt. Accessed 3 Apr. 2025.

Pew Research Center. *Many Americans Continue to Experience Mental Health Difficulties as Pandemic Enters Second Year*. 16 Mar. 2021, www.pewresearch.org/fact-tank/2021/03/16/many-americans-continue-to-experience-mental-health-difficulties-as-pandemic-enters-second-year/. Accessed 1 Dec. 2021.

Pokora, Becky. "Credit Card Statistics and Trends 2024." *Forbes Advisor*, n.d., https://www.forbes.com/advisor/credit-cards/credit-card-statistics/. Accessed 2 Apr. 2025.

Prelec, Drazen, and Duncan Simester. "Always Leave Home Without It: A Further Investigation of the Credit-Card Effect on Willingness to Pay." *Marketing Letters*, vol. 12, no. 1, Feb. 2001, pp. 5–12. Springer, https://doi.org/10.1023/A:1008196717017. Accessed 2 Apr. 2025.

"Dodd–Frank Wall Street Reform and Consumer Protection Act." Wikipedia, The Free Encyclopedia, Wikimedia Foundation, 1 Apr. 2025, https://en.wikipedia.org/wiki/Dodd%E2%80%93Frank_Wall_Street_Reform_and_Consumer_Protection_Act.

Federal Reserve Bank of New York. *Quarterly Report on Household Debt and Credit*. Federal Reserve Bank of New York, 2025, https://www.newyorkfed.org/microeconomics/hhdc.

"The History of Credit Cards." Experian, 9 Mar. 2024, www.experian.com/blogs/ask-experian/the-history-of-credit-cards/. Accessed 31 Mar. 2025.

Quinlan, Casey. "U.S. Credit Card Debt Rises as Housing and Other Costs Remain High." *Governing*, 4 Sept. 2024, https://www.governing.com/finance/u-s-credit-card-debt-rises-as-housing-and-other-costs-remain-high.

Seaman, Stephen. *History of the Credit Card. Swipesum*, 12 Sept. 2024, www.swipesum.com/insights/history-of-the-credit-card. Accessed 3 Apr. 2025.

Shukla, Shivam. "Overspending on Credit Cards? Here's the Psychology You Need to Understand." *Mint*, 17 Mar. 2025, https://www.livemint.com/money/personal-finance/overspending-on-credit-cards-heres-the-psychology-you-need-to-understand-11740467305697.html. Accessed 2 Apr. 2025.

Tsosie, Claire. "Why So Many of Your Credit Cards Come from Delaware." *NerdWallet*, 25 Mar. 2024, https://www.nerdwallet.com/article/credit-cards/why-so-many-of-your-credit-cards-come-from-delaware. Accessed 31 Mar. 2025.

Wikipedia. "Reaganomics." *Wikipedia, The Free Encyclopedia*, Wikimedia Foundation, https://en.wikipedia.org/wiki/Reaganomics#:~:text=Reaganomics%20(%2Fre%C9%AA%C9%A1%C9%99,Ronald%20Reagan%20during%20the%201980s. Accessed 4 Apr. 2025.

Wikipedia. "Banking in Ancient Rome." *Wikipedia, The Free Encyclopedia*, Wikimedia Foundation, https://en.wikipedia.org/wiki/

Banking_in_ancient_Rome#:~:text=Although%20these%20financial%20services%20were,in%20trade%20should%20use%20credit. Accessed 4 Apr. 2025.

www.ingramcontent.com/pod-product-compliance
Lightning Source LLC
LaVergne TN
LVHW022312200926
848481LV00004B/1295
9798295528231